MY RECIPE BOOKLET

Special Christmas

Summary

Page	Recipe name

Summary

Page	Recipe name

Summary

Page	Recipe name

Summary

Page	Recipe name

Summary

Page	Recipe name

Recipe _____

🌡 Temperature _____   ⏱ Cooking time _____

⏳ Preparation time _____   👤 Number of _____ parts

Paste a photo or draw

Ingredients	Preparation 🧑‍🍳

Notes _____

_____

_____

Difficulty 1 2 3 4 5 6 7 8 9 10

Recipe _____

Temperature _____   Cooking time _____

Preparation time _____   Number of _____
parts

Paste a photo or draw

Ingredients	Preparation

Notes _____

_____

_____

Difficulty 1 2 3 4 5 6 7 8 9 10

Recipe _____

Temperature _____   Cooking time _____

Preparation time _____   Number of _____
parts

Paste a photo or draw

Ingredients	Preparation 🧑‍🍳

Notes _____

_____

_____

Difficulty 1 2 3 4 5 6 7 8 9 10

Recipe _____

Temperature _____   **Cooking time** _____

Preparation time _____   **Number of** _____
parts

Paste a photo or draw

Ingredients	Preparation

Notes _____

_____

_____

Difficulty 1 2 3 4 5 6 7 8 9 10

Recipe _____

🌡 Temperature _____ ⏱ Cooking time _____

⏳ Preparation time _____ 👤 Number of _____
parts

Paste a photo or draw

Ingredients | Preparation 👨‍🍳

Notes _____

Difficulty 1 2 3 4 5 6 7 8 9 10

Recipe _____

🌡️ Temperature _____   ⏱️ Cooking time _____

⏳ Preparation time _____   👤 Number of _____
                                    parts

Paste a photo or draw

Ingredients	Preparation 👨‍🍳

Notes _____

_____

_____

Difficulty 1 2 3 4 5 6 7 8 9 10

Recipe _____

Temperature _____

Cooking time _____

Preparation time _____

Number of _____
parts

Paste a photo or draw

Ingredients	Preparation 🧑‍🍳

Notes _____

_____

_____

Difficulty 1 2 3 4 5 6 7 8 9 10

Recipe _____

Temperature _____   Cooking time _____

Preparation time _____   Number of _____
parts

Paste a photo or draw

Ingredients | Preparation 🧑‍🍳

_____

Notes _____

Difficulty 1 2 3 4 5 6 7 8 9 10

Recipe _____

Temperature _____ **Cooking time** _____

Preparation time _____ **Number of** _____
parts

Paste a photo or draw

Ingredients	Preparation

Notes _____

_____

_____

Difficulty 1 2 3 4 5 6 7 8 9 10

Recipe _____

Temperature _____   **Cooking time** _____

Preparation time _____   **Number of parts** _____

Paste a photo or draw

Ingredients | Preparation 👨‍🍳

🍬 Notes _____

_____

_____

Difficulty 1 2 3 4 5 6 7 8 9 10

Recipe _____

Temperature _____

Cooking time _____

Preparation time _____

Number of _____
parts

Paste a photo or draw

Ingredients	Preparation

Notes _____

_____

_____

Difficulty 1 2 3 4 5 6 7 8 9 10

Recipe _____

Temperature _____ **Cooking time** _____

Preparation time _____ **Number of parts** _____

Paste a photo or draw

Ingredients | Preparation 🧑‍🍳

_____

Notes _____

_____

_____

Difficulty 1 2 3 4 5 6 7 8 9 10

Recipe _____

🌡️ Temperature _____ ⏱️ Cooking time _____

⏳ Preparation time _____ 👤 Number of _____ parts

Paste a photo or draw
_____

Ingredients	Preparation

Notes _____

Difficulty 1 2 3 4 5 6 7 8 9 10

Recipe _____

Temperature _____ **Cooking time** _____

Preparation time _____ **Number of** _____
parts

Paste a photo or draw

Ingredients | Preparation 👨‍🍳

Notes _____

_____

_____

Difficulty 1 2 3 4 5 6 7 8 9 10

Recipe _____

Temperature _____   **Cooking time** _____

Preparation time _____   **Number of parts** _____

Paste a photo or draw

Ingredients | Preparation 🧑‍🍳

Notes _____

_____

_____

Difficulty 1 2 3 4 5 6 7 8 9 10

Recipe _____

Temperature _____   **Cooking time** _____

Preparation time _____   **Number of** _____
parts

Paste a photo or draw

Ingredients	Preparation 👨‍🍳

Notes _____

_____

_____

Difficulty 1 2 3 4 5 6 7 8 9 10

Recipe _____

Temperature _____   **Cooking time** _____

Preparation time _____   **Number of parts** _____

Paste a photo or draw

Ingredients	Preparation 👨‍🍳

Notes _____

_____

_____

Difficulty 1 2 3 4 5 6 7 8 9 10

Recipe _____

Temperature _____   **Cooking time** _____

Preparation time _____   **Number of parts** _____

Paste a photo or draw

Ingredients	Preparation 🧑‍🍳

Notes _____

_____

_____

Difficulty 1 2 3 4 5 6 7 8 9 10

Recipe _____

Temperature _____ Cooking time _____

Preparation time _____ Number of _____
parts

Paste a photo or draw

Ingredients	Preparation 👨‍🍳

Notes _____

_____

_____

Difficulty 1 2 3 4 5 6 7 8 9 10

Recipe _____

Temperature _____   **Cooking time** _____

Preparation time _____   **Number of parts** _____

Paste a photo or draw

Ingredients	Preparation 🧑‍🍳

Notes _____

_____

_____

Difficulty 1 2 3 4 5 6 7 8 9 10

Recipe _____

Temperature _____   Cooking time _____

Preparation time _____   Number of _____
parts

Paste a photo or draw

Ingredients	Preparation 🧑‍🍳

Notes _____ 🥣

_____

_____

Difficulty 1 2 3 4 5 6 7 8 9 10

Recipe _____

Temperature _____   **Cooking time** _____

Preparation time _____   **Number of** _____
parts

Paste a photo or draw

Ingredients | Preparation 🧑‍🍳

_____

Notes _____

_____

_____

Difficulty 1 2 3 4 5 6 7 8 9 10

Recipe _____

Temperature _____

Cooking time _____

Preparation time _____

Number of parts _____

Paste a photo or draw

Ingredients | Preparation

Notes _____

Difficulty 1 2 3 4 5 6 7 8 9 10

Recipe _____

Temperature _____   **Cooking time** _____

Preparation time _____   **Number of** _____
parts

Paste a photo or draw

Ingredients	Preparation 🧑‍🍳

Notes _____ 🥣

_____

_____

Difficulty 1 2 3 4 5 6 7 8 9 10

Recipe _____

🌡️ Temperature _____   ⏱️ Cooking time _____

⏳ Preparation time _____   👤 Number of _____
parts

Paste a photo or draw

Ingredients | Preparation

Notes _____

_____

_____

Difficulty 1 2 3 4 5 6 7 8 9 10

Recipe _____

Temperature _____   Cooking time _____

Preparation time _____   Number of _____ parts

Paste a photo or draw

Ingredients	Preparation 👨‍🍳

Notes _____

_____

Difficulty 1 2 3 4 5 6 7 8 9 10

Recipe _____

Temperature _____   Cooking time _____

Preparation time _____   Number of _____
parts

Paste a photo or draw

Ingredients	Preparation

Notes _____

_____

_____

Difficulty 1 2 3 4 5 6 7 8 9 10

Recipe _____

Temperature _____ **Cooking time** _____

Preparation time _____ **Number of** _____
parts

Paste a photo or draw

Ingredients | Preparation 🧑‍🍳

Notes _____

Difficulty 1 2 3 4 5 6 7 8 9 10

Recipe _____

Temperature _____   **Cooking time** _____

Preparation time _____   **Number of** _____
parts

Paste a photo or draw

Ingredients	Preparation

Notes _____

_____

_____

Difficulty *1 2 3 4 5 6 7 8 9 10*

Recipe _____

🌡️ Temperature _____   ⏱️ Cooking time _____

⏳ Preparation time _____   👤 Number of _____
                                      parts

Paste a photo or draw

Ingredients	Preparation

Notes _____

_____

_____

Difficulty 1 2 3 4 5 6 7 8 9 10

Recipe _____

Temperature _____   Cooking time _____

Preparation time _____   Number of _____
parts

Paste a photo or draw

Ingredients	Preparation 🧑‍🍳

Notes _____

_____

_____

Difficulty 1 2 3 4 5 6 7 8 9 10

Recipe _____

Temperature _____

Cooking time _____

Preparation time _____

Number of parts _____

Paste a photo or draw

Ingredients	Preparation 🧑‍🍳

Notes _____ 🥣

_____

_____

Difficulty 1 2 3 4 5 6 7 8 9 10

Recipe _____

Temperature _____   **Cooking time** _____

Preparation time _____   **Number of _____ parts**

Paste a photo or draw

Ingredients | Preparation

_____

Notes _____

Difficulty 1 2 3 4 5 6 7 8 9 10

Recipe _____

Temperature _____   **Cooking time** _____

Preparation time _____   **Number of parts** _____

Paste a photo or draw

Ingredients | Preparation 👨‍🍳

Notes _____

Difficulty 1 2 3 4 5 6 7 8 9 10

Recipe _____

🌡 Temperature _____   ⏱ Cooking time _____

⏳ Preparation time _____   👤 Number of _____ parts

Paste a photo or draw

Ingredients	Preparation

Notes _____

_____

_____

Difficulty 1 2 3 4 5 6 7 8 9 10

Recipe _____

Temperature _____   Cooking time _____

Preparation time _____   Number of _____
parts

Paste a photo or draw

Ingredients | Preparation 👨‍🍳

_____

_____

_____

_____

_____

_____

_____

_____

_____

_____

Notes _____

_____

_____

Difficulty 1 2 3 4 5 6 7 8 9 10

Recipe _____

Temperature _____   **Cooking time** _____

Preparation time _____   **Number of** _____
parts

Paste a photo or draw

Ingredients	Preparation 👨‍🍳

Notes _____

_____

_____

Difficulty 1 2 3 4 5 6 7 8 9 10

Recipe _____

Temperature _____ **Cooking time** _____

Preparation time _____ **Number of parts** _____

Paste a photo or draw

Ingredients	Preparation 🧑‍🍳

Notes _____

_____

_____

Difficulty 1 2 3 4 5 6 7 8 9 10

Recipe _____

Temperature _____ **Cooking time** _____

Preparation time _____ **Number of** _____
parts

Paste a photo or draw

Ingredients	Preparation

Notes _____

_____

_____

Difficulty 1 2 3 4 5 6 7 8 9 10

Recipe _____

Temperature _____   **Cooking time** _____

Preparation time _____   **Number of parts** _____

Paste a photo or draw

Ingredients | Preparation 🧑‍🍳

Notes _____

_____

_____

Difficulty 1 2 3 4 5 6 7 8 9 10

Recipe _____

Temperature _____   Cooking time _____

Preparation time _____   Number of _____ parts

Paste a photo or draw

Ingredients	Preparation 🧑‍🍳

Notes _____

_____

_____

Difficulty 1 2 3 4 5 6 7 8 9 10

Recipe _____

Temperature _____ **Cooking time** _____

Preparation time _____ **Number of parts** _____

Paste a photo or draw

Ingredients	Preparation

Notes _____

_____

_____

Difficulty 1 2 3 4 5 6 7 8 9 10

Recipe _____

Temperature _____

Cooking time _____

Preparation time _____

Number of _____
parts

Paste a photo or draw

Ingredients	Preparation 🧑‍🍳

Notes _____

_____

_____

Difficulty 1 2 3 4 5 6 7 8 9 10

Recipe _____

Temperature _____ **Cooking time** _____

Preparation time _____ **Number of parts** _____

Paste a photo or draw

Ingredients	Preparation 🧑‍🍳

Notes _____

_____

_____

Difficulty 1 2 3 4 5 6 7 8 9 10

Recipe _____

Temperature _____   **Cooking time** _____

Preparation time _____   **Number of** _____
parts

Paste a photo or draw

Ingredients	Preparation 👨‍🍳

Notes _____ 🥣

_____

_____

Difficulty 1 2 3 4 5 6 7 8 9 10

Recipe _____

Temperature _____   Cooking time _____

Preparation time _____   Number of _____
parts

Paste a photo or draw

Ingredients	Preparation 🧑‍🍳

Notes _____

_____

_____

Difficulty 1 2 3 4 5 6 7 8 9 10

Recipe _____

🌡 Temperature _____   ⏱ Cooking time _____

⏳ Preparation time _____   👤 Number of _____ parts

Paste a photo or draw

Ingredients	Preparation

Notes _____

_____

_____

Difficulty 1 2 3 4 5 6 7 8 9 10

Recipe _____

Temperature _____   **Cooking time** _____

Preparation time _____   **Number of** _____
parts

Paste a photo or draw

Ingredients	Preparation 🧑‍🍳

Notes _____

_____

_____

Difficulty 1 2 3 4 5 6 7 8 9 10

Recipe _____

🌡️ Temperature _____ ⏱️ Cooking time _____

⏳ Preparation time _____ 👤 Number of _____
parts

Paste a photo or draw

Ingredients	Preparation 🧑‍🍳

Notes _____ 🥣

_____

_____

Difficulty 1 2 3 4 5 6 7 8 9 10

Recipe _____

Temperature _____   Cooking time _____

Preparation time _____   Number of _____
parts

Paste a photo or draw

Ingredients	Preparation

Notes _____

_____

_____

Difficulty 1 2 3 4 5 6 7 8 9 10

Recipe _____

Temperature _____   Cooking time _____

Preparation time _____   Number of _____ parts

Paste a photo or draw

Ingredients	Preparation 🧑‍🍳

Notes _____

_____

_____

Difficulty 1 2 3 4 5 6 7 8 9 10

Recipe _____

🌡️ Temperature _____   ⏱️ Cooking time _____

⏳ Preparation time _____   👤 Number of _____
parts

Paste a photo or draw

Ingredients	Preparation

Notes _____

_____

Difficulty 1 2 3 4 5 6 7 8 9 10

Recipe _____

Temperature _____ Cooking time _____

Preparation time _____ Number of _____ parts

Paste a photo or draw

Ingredients	Preparation

Notes _____

_____

_____

Difficulty 1 2 3 4 5 6 7 8 9 10

Recipe _____

Temperature _____   **Cooking time** _____

Preparation time _____   **Number of** _____
parts

Paste a photo or draw

Ingredients	Preparation 🧑‍🍳

Notes _____

_____

_____

Difficulty 1 2 3 4 5 6 7 8 9 10

Recipe _____

🌡️ Temperature _____   ⏱️ Cooking time _____

⏳ Preparation time _____   👤 Number of _____
                                    parts

Paste a photo or draw

Ingredients	Preparation

Notes _____

_____

_____

Difficulty 1 2 3 4 5 6 7 8 9 10

Recipe _____

Temperature _____ **Cooking time** _____

Preparation time _____ **Number of parts** _____

Paste a photo or draw

Ingredients | Preparation

_____

Notes _____

_____

_____

Difficulty 1 2 3 4 5 6 7 8 9 10

Recipe _____

Temperature _____   **Cooking time** _____

Preparation time _____   **Number of** _____
parts

Paste a photo or draw

Ingredients	Preparation

Notes _____

_____

_____

Difficulty 1 2 3 4 5 6 7 8 9 10

Recipe _____

Temperature _____   **Cooking time** _____

Preparation time _____   **Number of parts** _____

Paste a photo or draw

Ingredients	Preparation 🧑‍🍳

Notes _____

_____

_____

Difficulty 1 2 3 4 5 6 7 8 9 10

Recipe _____

Temperature _____ **Cooking time** _____

Preparation time _____ **Number of parts** _____

Paste a photo or draw

Ingredients	Preparation 🧑‍🍳

🎄 Notes _____ 🥣

_____

_____

Difficulty 1 2 3 4 5 6 7 8 9 10

Recipe _____

Temperature _____ **Cooking time** _____

Preparation time _____ **Number of** _____
parts

Paste a photo or draw

Ingredients | Preparation 👨‍🍳

Notes _____

Difficulty 1 2 3 4 5 6 7 8 9 10

Recipe _____

🌡️ Temperature _____   ⏱️ Cooking time _____

⏳ Preparation time _____   👤 Number of _____
parts

Paste a photo or draw

Ingredients	Preparation 🧑‍🍳

Notes _____

_____

_____

Difficulty 1 2 3 4 5 6 7 8 9 10

Recipe _____

🌡️ Temperature _____ ⏱️ Cooking time _____

⏳ Preparation time _____ 👤 Number of _____ parts

Paste a photo or draw

Ingredients	Preparation

Notes _____

_____

_____

Difficulty 1 2 3 4 5 6 7 8 9 10

Recipe _____

Temperature _____ **Cooking time** _____

Preparation time _____ **Number of parts** _____

Paste a photo or draw

Ingredients | Preparation

(blank recipe card)

Notes _____

_____

_____

Difficulty 1 2 3 4 5 6 7 8 9 10

Recipe _____

Temperature _____   **Cooking time** _____

Preparation time _____   **Number of** _____
parts

Paste a photo or draw

Ingredients	Preparation 🧑‍🍳

Notes _____

_____

_____

Difficulty 1 2 3 4 5 6 7 8 9 10

Recipe _____

Temperature _____

Cooking time _____

Preparation time _____

Number of _____
parts

Paste a photo or draw

Ingredients	Preparation 👨‍🍳

Notes _____

_____

_____

Difficulty 1 2 3 4 5 6 7 8 9 10

Recipe _____

Temperature _____   Cooking time _____

Preparation time _____   Number of parts _____

Paste a photo or draw

Ingredients	Preparation 🧑‍🍳

Notes _____

_____

_____

Difficulty 1 2 3 4 5 6 7 8 9 10

Recipe _____

🌡️ Temperature _____   ⏱️ Cooking time _____

⏳ Preparation time _____   👤 Number of _____
                                    parts

Paste a photo or draw

Ingredients	Preparation 🧑‍🍳

Notes _____

_____

_____

Difficulty 1 2 3 4 5 6 7 8 9 10

Recipe _____

🌡️ Temperature _____ ⏱️ Cooking time _____

⏳ Preparation time _____ 👤 Number of parts _____

Paste a photo or draw

Ingredients | Preparation

Notes

Difficulty 1 2 3 4 5 6 7 8 9 10

Recipe _____

🌡 Temperature _____ ⏱ Cooking time _____

⏳ Preparation time _____ 👤 Number of _____ parts

Paste a photo or draw

Ingredients	Preparation

Notes _____

_____

_____

Difficulty 1 2 3 4 5 6 7 8 9 10

Recipe _____

Temperature _____

Cooking time _____

Preparation time _____

Number of parts _____

Paste a photo or draw

Ingredients	Preparation

Notes _____

_____

_____

Difficulty 1 2 3 4 5 6 7 8 9 10

Recipe _____

Temperature _____   **Cooking time** _____

Preparation time _____   **Number of parts** _____

Paste a photo or draw

Ingredients	Preparation

Notes _____

_____

_____

Difficulty 1 2 3 4 5 6 7 8 9 10

Recipe _____

🌡 Temperature _____   ⏱ Cooking time _____

⏳ Preparation time _____   👤 Number of _____ parts

Paste a photo or draw

Ingredients	Preparation 🧑‍🍳

🥢 Notes _____ 🥣

_____

_____

Difficulty 1 2 3 4 5 6 7 8 9 10

Recipe _____

Temperature _____ **Cooking time** _____

Preparation time _____ **Number of** _____
parts

Paste a photo or draw

Ingredients | Preparation 👨‍🍳

_____

_____

_____

_____

_____

_____

_____

_____

_____

Notes _____

_____

_____

Difficulty 1 2 3 4 5 6 7 8 9 10

Recipe _____

Temperature _____   **Cooking time** _____

Preparation time _____   **Number of parts** _____

Paste a photo or draw

Ingredients	Preparation 🧑‍🍳

Notes _____

_____

_____

Difficulty 1 2 3 4 5 6 7 8 9 10

Recipe _____

Temperature _____   Cooking time _____

Preparation time _____   Number of _____
parts

Paste a photo or draw

Ingredients	Preparation 🧑‍🍳

Notes _____

_____

_____

Difficulty 1 2 3 4 5 6 7 8 9 10

Recipe _____

Temperature _____   **Cooking time** _____

Preparation time _____   **Number of parts** _____

Paste a photo or draw

Ingredients | Preparation

Notes _____

_____

_____

Difficulty 1 2 3 4 5 6 7 8 9 10

Recipe _____

Temperature _____

Cooking time _____

Preparation time _____

Number of parts _____

Paste a photo or draw

Ingredients	Preparation 🧑‍🍳

Notes _____

_____

_____

Difficulty 1 2 3 4 5 6 7 8 9 10

Recipe _____

Temperature _____   Cooking time _____

Preparation time _____   Number of _____
                                         parts

Paste a photo or draw

Ingredients	Preparation

Notes _____

_____

_____

Difficulty 1 2 3 4 5 6 7 8 9 10

Recipe _____

Temperature _____ **Cooking time** _____

Preparation time _____ **Number of** _____
parts

Paste a photo or draw

Ingredients	Preparation 🧑‍🍳

Notes _____

_____

_____

Difficulty 1 2 3 4 5 6 7 8 9 10

Recipe _____

Temperature _____ **Cooking time** _____

Preparation time _____ **Number of parts** _____

Paste a photo or draw

Ingredients	Preparation 👨‍🍳

Notes _____

_____

_____

Difficulty 1 2 3 4 5 6 7 8 9 10

Recipe _____

Temperature _____   Cooking time _____

Preparation time _____   Number of _____
parts

Paste a photo or draw

Ingredients	Preparation 🧑‍🍳

🎄 **Notes** _____ 🥣

_____

_____

Difficulty 1 2 3 4 5 6 7 8 9 10

Recipe _____

Temperature _____   Cooking time _____

Preparation time _____   Number of _____
                                parts

Paste a photo or draw

Ingredients	Preparation

Notes _____

_____

_____

Difficulty 1 2 3 4 5 6 7 8 9 10

Recipe _____

Temperature _____ **Cooking time** _____

Preparation time _____ **Number of parts** _____

Paste a photo or draw

Ingredients	Preparation 🧑‍🍳

Notes _____

_____

_____

Difficulty 1 2 3 4 5 6 7 8 9 10

Recipe _____

Temperature _____ **Cooking time** _____

Preparation time _____ **Number of parts** _____

Paste a photo or draw

Ingredients	Preparation 🧑‍🍳

Notes _____

_____

_____

Difficulty 1 2 3 4 5 6 7 8 9 10

Recipe _____

Temperature _____   **Cooking time** _____

Preparation time _____   **Number of** _____
parts

Paste a photo or draw

Ingredients	Preparation

Notes _____

_____

_____

Difficulty 1 2 3 4 5 6 7 8 9 10

Recipe _____

Temperature _____

Cooking time _____

Preparation time _____

Number of parts _____

Paste a photo or draw

Ingredients	Preparation

Notes _____

_____

_____

Difficulty 1 2 3 4 5 6 7 8 9 10

Recipe _____

Temperature _____ **Cooking time** _____

Preparation time _____ **Number of** _____
parts

Paste a photo or draw

Ingredients	Preparation

Notes _____

_____

_____

Difficulty 1 2 3 4 5 6 7 8 9 10

Recipe _____

🌡 Temperature _____   ⏱ Cooking time _____

⏳ Preparation time _____   👤 Number of _____ parts

Paste a photo or draw

Ingredients	Preparation 👨‍🍳

Notes _____

_____

_____

Difficulty 1 2 3 4 5 6 7 8 9 10

Recipe _____

Temperature _____   Cooking time _____

Preparation time _____   Number of _____
parts

Paste a photo or draw

Ingredients	Preparation 👨‍🍳

Notes _____

_____

_____

Difficulty 1 2 3 4 5 6 7 8 9 10

Recipe _____

Temperature _____   Cooking time _____

Preparation time _____   Number of _____
parts

Paste a photo or draw

Ingredients	Preparation

Notes _____

_____

_____

Difficulty 1 2 3 4 5 6 7 8 9 10

Recipe _____

Temperature _____ **Cooking time** _____

Preparation time _____ **Number of parts** _____

Paste a photo or draw

Ingredients	Preparation 🧑‍🍳

Notes _____

_____

_____

Difficulty 1 2 3 4 5 6 7 8 9 10

Recipe _____

🌡 Temperature _____   ⏱ Cooking time _____

⏳ Preparation time _____   👤 Number of _____
parts

Paste a photo or draw

Ingredients	Preparation 🧑‍🍳

Notes _____

_____

_____

Difficulty 1 2 3 4 5 6 7 8 9 10

Recipe _____

🌡 Temperature _____   ⏱ Cooking time _____

⏳ Preparation time _____   👤 Number of _____ parts

Paste a photo or draw

Ingredients	Preparation 🧑‍🍳

Notes _____

_____

_____

Difficulty 1 2 3 4 5 6 7 8 9 10

Recipe _____

Temperature _____ Cooking time _____

Preparation time _____ Number of _____
parts

Paste a photo or draw

Ingredients	Preparation 🧑‍🍳

Notes _____

_____

_____

Difficulty 1 2 3 4 5 6 7 8 9 10

Recipe _____

Temperature _____   **Cooking time** _____

Preparation time _____   **Number of** _____
parts

Paste a photo or draw

Ingredients	Preparation 🧑‍🍳

Notes _____

_____

_____

Difficulty 1 2 3 4 5 6 7 8 9 10

Recipe _____

Temperature _____   **Cooking time** _____

Preparation time _____   **Number of parts** _____

Paste a photo or draw

Ingredients	Preparation 🧑‍🍳

Notes _____

_____

_____

Difficulty 1 2 3 4 5 6 7 8 9 10

Recipe _____

Temperature _____ Cooking time _____

Preparation time _____ Number of _____
parts

Paste a photo or draw

Ingredients	Preparation

Notes _____

_____

_____

Difficulty 1 2 3 4 5 6 7 8 9 10

Recipe _____

Temperature _____   Cooking time _____

Preparation time _____   Number of _____
parts

Paste a photo or draw

Ingredients	Preparation 🧑‍🍳

Notes _____

_____

_____

Difficulty 1 2 3 4 5 6 7 8 9 10

Recipe _____

Temperature _____   Cooking time _____

Preparation time _____   Number of _____
parts

Paste a photo or draw

Ingredients	Preparation

Notes _____

_____

_____

Difficulty 1 2 3 4 5 6 7 8 9 10

Recipe _____

Temperature _____ **Cooking time** _____

Preparation time _____ **Number of parts** _____

Paste a photo or draw

Ingredients	Preparation

Notes _____

_____

_____

Difficulty 1 2 3 4 5 6 7 8 9 10

Made in the USA
Monee, IL
29 November 2023

47711543R00114